WITHDRAWN

MANNERS
WITH FRIENDS

JOSH PLATTNER

Consulting Editor, Diane Craig, M.A./Reading Specialist

Sandcastle

An Imprint of Abdo Publishing
abdopublishing.com

abdopublishing.com

Published by Abdo Publishing, a division of ABDO, PO Box 398166, Minneapolis, Minnesota 55439. Copyright © 2016 by Abdo Consulting Group, Inc. International copyrights reserved in all countries. No part of this book may be reproduced in any form without written permission from the publisher. SandCastle™ is a trademark and logo of Abdo Publishing.

Printed in the United States of America, North Mankato, Minnesota
062015
092015

THIS BOOK CONTAINS RECYCLED MATERIALS

Editor: Alex Kuskowski
Content Developer: Nancy Tuminelly
Cover and Interior Design and Production: Mighty Media, Inc.
Photo Credits: Shutterstock

Library of Congress Cataloging-in-Publication Data
Plattner, Josh, author.
  Manners with friends / Josh Plattner ; consulting editor, Diane Craig, M.A./reading specialist.
     pages cm. -- (Manners)
  Audience: PreK to grade 3.
  ISBN 978-1-62403-719-1
1. Friendship--Juvenile literature. 2. Etiquette for children and teenagers. I. Title.
  BJ1857.C5P53 62016
  177.62--dc23
              2014046313

SandCastle™ Level: Transitional

SandCastle™ books are created by a team of professional educators, reading specialists, and content developers around five essential components—phonemic awareness, phonics, vocabulary, text comprehension, and fluency—to assist young readers as they develop reading skills and strategies and increase their general knowledge. All books are written, reviewed, and leveled for guided reading, early reading intervention, and Accelerated Reader™ programs for use in shared, guided, and independent reading and writing activities to support a balanced approach to literacy instruction. The SandCastle™ series has four levels that correspond to early literacy development. The levels are provided to help teachers and parents select appropriate books for young readers.

EMERGING · BEGINNING · **TRANSITIONAL** · FLUENT

CONTENTS

MANNERS WITH FRIENDS

Manners are great! They are important.
Use them with your friends.

SIMPLY SMILE

Liz smiles when she is having fun. It makes her look happy. Her smile helps her friends smile more.

SHAKING HANDS

Ben shakes his new friend's hand. It is polite. He doesn't **squeeze** too tight.

GIVING HUGS

Hugs are great! They comfort our friends. Hugs also help us say hello and goodbye.

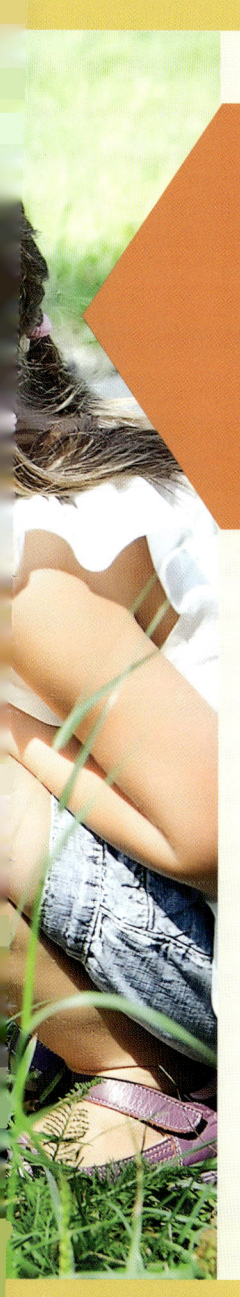

SAYING SORRY

Did you hurt your
friend's feelings?
Say you are sorry. Be
honest. Be respectful.

C'MON OVER!

Tina invites her friend home after school. Tina asks her parents first. She makes sure it's okay to have friends over.

HELPFUL HANDS

Dan knows when his
friends need help.
He pays attention.
He helps however
he can.

FUN AND GAMES

Find something everyone wants to play. Try a new activity. Make sure everyone is having fun.

BIG DIFFERENCES

No one is exactly the same. Respect each other's **differences**. It will help you make more friends.

KEEP IT UP!

Always practice good manners with your friends. Can you think of more? What else could you do?

GLOSSARY

difference – the way in which people or things are not alike.

squeeze – to press the sides of something together.